Epiphany
Or
Sin

Based on a true story

Elvis Slaughter

Elvis Slaughter

Dedication

This book is dedicated to my mom and those who treated me
like a son—those who have nurtured and looked over me
since childhood:

Acknowledgment

I want to thank all of my siblings for all they have done for Mom throughout the years, as well as the countless number of relatives and friends who gave their support.

Personal Note

Throughout my life, I have felt in tune with the energy of the universe and insight through a divine connection. I have experienced clairvoyance at least five times. In four of these instances, it prevented me from walking into danger. I also believe in the power of words. I believe I was chosen to tell this story long before it occurred. Now I have closure. I kept the story short to bring focus to the importance of the problems of tainted blood and the hope of a possible solution.

To Mother: I love you!

Preface

Epiphany or Sin was inspired by the true story of my mother's death. During the investigation of my mother's death, many questions were asked. How was she killed? Who is at fault? After reviewing the FDA's relevant information concerning the blood companies' involvement, my mother's ordeal, and her medical records, I am convinced that there might have been sin in a murder and a cover-up. My spiritual experiences led me to also believe that thousands of people died after receiving tainted blood transfusions between 1991 and 1996 and today. This journal is a testimony of my divine appointment to tell my mom's personal story, which is linked to the worldwide HIV/AIDS epidemic. It includes accounts showing that approximately forty thousand or more people were affected by tainted blood transfusions; many of them are believed to have become sick and died. My mother was among one of those believed to be infected when she was transfused with blood at South Shore and Columbus hospitals in Chicago, Illinois.

Epiphany or Sin is based on a true story. It is the investigational record of my mother's tragic death, which occurred after she was transfused with what was believed to be tainted blood products. The infected blood caused viral infections associated with AIDS, hepatitis, leukemia, sepsis, and led, eventually, to death. At one point, I was told that my mother had been diagnosed with and was being treated for Wegener's granulomatosis. This rare disorder causes inflammation of blood vessels (vasculitis) in the upper respiratory tract (nose, sinuses, and ears), lungs, and kidneys. I later learned that her doctors had prescribed medications that treat not only Wegener's granulomatosis, but hepatitis and leukemia as well.

A newspaper article stated that over forty thousand people had been affected in some way by the adulterated blood products, but the victims were never notified; and it wasn't until two years later, in that article, that they discovered the truth.

Many of those infected may have died, and the statute of limitations—a law assigning a certain length of time for prosecution, after which rights cannot be enforced by legal action or offenses punished—had expired by the time the notice appeared in the newspaper. Was it a cover-up, or was it coincidental that a lawsuit claiming a patient had been given tainted blood, contracted AIDS, and eventually died was being heard in the Illinois Supreme Court at the same time?

Elvis Slaughter

The following newspaper article and the transcript of a recorded voicemail message from a South Shore Hospital doctor give insight into what I believe contributed to my mother's death. It's possible that there are thousands of other victims, which shows the severity of the tainted blood crisis. Evidential documents in part 1 and part 2 of this narrative indicate that the blood supply was tainted before 1994.

Flawed Screening Raises Concerns Over Blood Safety
December 2, 1998
(Chicago Tribune)
An estimated thirty-five to forty thousand people may have received tainted blood transfusions or supplies at twenty-eight Chicago-area hospitals between June 1994 and December 1996. The blood may not have been properly tested for HIV or hepatitis viruses.
Four Cities Alerted

The faulty testing was performed by the New York Blood Center, which screens blood for United Blood Services (UBS). While UBS provided blood supplies to hospitals in eighteen states, only blood sent to hospitals in Chicago, Pittsburgh, Memphis, and New York was affected.

What Happened?

1. New York Blood Center technicians exposed blood samples to chemicals that reacted to viral antibodies carried by infected blood.

2

2. A second test was to be performed using a control sample of chemicals to ensure the testing procedure was accurate.

3. It is believed that the testing lab may not have renewed the control samples frequently enough, putting the accuracy of the entire screening process in doubt.

The flawed procedures were uncovered in late 1996, after an FDA investigation.

Screening Blood

Since 1985, blood is tested for:

1. HIV antigen, HIV-1, and HIV-2 (HIV is the virus that causes AIDS)
2. HTLV (a bloodborne virus that can cause leukemia)
3. Hepatitis B and hepatitis C (viral infections that cause liver disease)

Samples showing any of these diseases are discarded.

The Illinois Department of Public Health records indicate that over fifteen thousand people were infected with AIDS alone between 1990 and 1999 in the Chicago and Cook County areas. These numbers showed an elevation between 1992 and 1996.

Voicemail Message:

Mr. Slaughter, this is Dr. —— from the laboratory at South Shore Hospital, returning your call. I did as much investigating as I could. As I

3

told you before, it doesn't look like we will be able to find out much. LifeSource and the New York Blood Service say there's no way to trace the donor of this particular unit, because it happened so long ago and because of the tremendous volume of units affected. It's overwhelming. As I told you before, if you have any questions about the medical situation, you need to talk to your mom's doctor, who I believe you told me was Dr. D——. I can give you his office number: 773-731——. And I did give him your name and number the last time we talked. I thought he was going to follow up with a phone call to you. I don't know if he has or not. But if you have any medical questions, that's who you need to be talking to. Thanks for your callback. See you later.

These incidents are just two of many events. Our family was devastated to learn that Mom had been a possible tainted blood victim. We began to recall incidents at the hospitals that correlated with the tainted blood recall. At that point, I set out to seek the truth and devoted all of the remaining insurance money to that cause.

Could a victim of the tainted blood crisis speak from the grave? I remember my first experience with the supernatural. I believe sharing this episode will allow you to understand how this story unfolded, and how my experience with the supernatural granted me an open mind on a subject from which many shy away. It was many years ago, the autumn of 1963. I was about four years old and living in the small southern town of Hollandale, Mississippi. My family toiled as sharecroppers on a plantation. The plantation was adjacent to an old graveyard.

One day, while my family tended the fields, I was walking on a beautiful tree-lined path, picking nuts, when I came upon a Godly, soldier-like figure on a horse. Horse and rider were enveloped in a white glow. The rider reached his hand out to me, and I reached out to him. At that moment, I felt a rush of energy go through my body. I was too young to understand what I had encountered, but I never forgot it.

That moment, though brief, was powerful, and the energy of it remained with me throughout my life. The best way to describe it is an adrenaline rush, or what Michael Jordan exhibits when he is in his groove on the basketball court. That same year, my mom decided to leave Hollandale, seeking a better life for us and leaving my father behind. It was a tough decision for her to make. The trip to Chicago was one of the longest car rides of my life, and that holds true to this day. Traveling that dark highway, cramped under my eight siblings, wasn't comfortable.

I still recall stopping at restaurants and rest stations and seeing signs that stated "Whites Only", "Negro Only", and "Colored Only". In Chicago, the rugged fields and memories of Hollandale became a piece of history. My mother was delighted. Her desire to protect and provide for us compelled her to become one of the craftiest seamstresses in the city of Chicago, drawing customers to her in droves. She was kindhearted and attractive, and she created many of our dress clothes from scratch. Until her health failed, we met at Mom's home to enjoy great Southern-style, home-cooked meals.

Forty years later, on October 9, 2004, I returned to Hollandale with my eighty-two-year-old uncle so that he might search for his brother, whom he hadn't seen in fifty years. It had been a long time since either of us had been home. Several phone calls later, we found my uncle's brother. I returned to that tree-lined path. While the rider did not reappear, I felt that same rush of energy. Often, while investigating my mother's death, this rush of energy led me to facts that would have otherwise escaped me.

In September of 1996, my mother, Mary, was admitted to South Shore Hospital. The doctors said her situation was not serious, but that she did have a heart condition. They indicated that they might have to perform a routine procedure to free one of her heart valves. The cardiologist said my mom would have to undergo a blood transfusion. My sisters and I didn't like the idea, but the cardiologist insisted it was necessary—otherwise, she would continue to weaken.

On October 6 and 7, 1996, Mom was given blood transfusions at South Shore Hospital. On October 8, 1996, she was transferred from South Shore to Columbus Hospital for further testing. Mom almost died that day as bacteria invaded her body and caused an infection. I learned that later, as we, her family, were not given that information at the time. When the doctor told us she needed a transfusion, I felt an energy flood my body, which caused me to resist his suggestion. But the doctor insisted and ultimately prevailed, and the procedure was done. In retrospect, I wish I had continued to resist. When the infection set in, Mom's cardiologist, Dr. Tyson, and her attending physician, Dr. Dayon, appeared as shocked and surprised as we were that she had taken a turn for the worse. One of my sisters stayed with her at the hospital, but those of us with less-accommodating employers had to be satisfied with visiting Mom daily until she was discharged. We were told that Mom had a disease called Wegener's granulomatosis. This was hard to believe, as it is rare in African-Americans; but her symptoms, including kidney failure, fit the disease.

On January 18, 1997, Mom was admitted to St. Margaret's Hospital in Hammond, Indiana, and referred to a clinic for dialysis. She underwent many tests while there. The test results revealed she had a *Staphylococcus aureus* bacterial infection, a dangerous condition because it is resistant to antibiotics. Although Mom continued to receive dialysis and treatment for Wegener's granulomatosis, her condition worsened. It seemed odd that the other infections identified earlier weren't detected at St. Margaret's Hospital, but perhaps they were suppressed by the medications she was taking. A short time later, she was admitted to South Suburban Hospital in Hazelcrest, Illinois. At South Suburban, the doctors were puzzled by her condition. The attending physicians were from Columbus Hospital, where she had received some of her blood transfusions. I became suspicious when a doctor told me, after I asked about her extended stay, that some of her medical expenses were being paid for by another source. Believing the charges were being paid by one of her previous doctors, I attempted to locate the source, but was unsuccessful. On March 24, 1997, while on my way to work, a notion came over me to check in on Mom. I detoured from my route and went to South Suburban. The staff was very courteous and allowed me immediate access. When I got off the elevator, a strange feeling came over me and I hurried to her room, expecting the worst. She was sitting up in bed, smiling, and seasoning her lunch. I hadn't seen her that energetic in months!

"Mom, how are you?" I asked.

"I'm great. The doctor said if I eat well, I can go home tomorrow."

"Oh, really?" I said.

I was stunned to see how happy she looked. She was glowing in her neat two-piece pajama set. I was amazed, but it felt so good to see her looking well that I believed she was going to be all right. I had to get to work, so I gave Mom a hug and a kiss on the cheek, and I told her I loved her. I went to work feeling great.

Early the next day, before sunrise, on March 25, 1997, the telephone rang. It was my sister. She said, "The hospital called and said Mom isn't doing so well. We need to get there right away." I sensed what was about to happen, but I wanted to think positively. I was hoping for the best. When I arrived at the hospital thirty minutes later, I went numb at the sound of people crying in my mother's room.

Mom was gone. As we all wept around her lifeless body, I felt her spirit near me. We all knew the pain she had endured since being hospitalized at South Shore. While we were relieved that her suffering was over, the question lingered in our minds: why did our mother die?

Who, or what, alerted me to visit Mother the day before she died? Did she know she was going to die? She had said, "I am going home tomorrow." What did she mean by "going home"?
A few days after my mother's funeral, I received a letter saying I had been accepted into Cooley Law School. I was very happy but felt sad, because although my mother had attended my high school and college graduations, she would never see me graduate from law school—a goal I had been working toward for several years. Two months later, I received a promotion at my job. However, my mother's death left me unable to take much pleasure in that either. Then, oddly enough, I found

myself attending more than twenty additional funerals, and my daughter had to have back surgery that summer.

While she was learning to walk again, I decided to prioritize my life. At that moment, my family was more important than school. I put off studying law for the time being. Instead, I used money that would have been spent for law school to finance my children's educations. I was so happy when 1997 ended; I had never had a year like it before. Some good things had happened; but losing my mother, having my daughter undergo back surgery, and dealing with so much death caused me to hope things would get better.

Epiphany or Sin

Early in the morning of December 2, 1998, I awoke from a dream and saw a beautiful full moon shining through the window. A familiar rush of energy surged through me, and gazing at the moon, I remembered my dream. I knew something important would be in the newspaper that morning, but I didn't really understand what was going on and fell back to sleep. I woke again around seven-thirty. I got my two daughters up for school, and then went outside to retrieve the newspaper. I took it with me to the kitchen, where my coffee was waiting. The headline stunned me: "Years Later, 40,000 Warned of Possible Transfusion Risk."

As I read the story, the mystery of my mother's death became clear. The article listed the years when people were infected and the hospitals where the individuals involved had been treated. Sure enough, South Shore and Columbus, where my mother had received her transfusions, were among those included. I immediately went to South Shore Hospital and demanded my mother's medical records. I then ordered the records from Columbus Hospital. After receiving and reviewing them, it seemed clear that Mom had become sick after her blood transfusions. According to her records, she had suffered more severely at Columbus than at South Shore.

Mom had received blood transfusions on November 6, 9, 10, 13, and 15, 1996, at Columbus Hospital. It was possible that she had received contaminated blood during those transfusions that would explain her relapses. Were the doctors unaware that the blood was polluted, or did they know and performed the multiple blood transfusions to try to cleanse her body of tainted blood? The newspaper stated the blood products concerned were administered between 1994 and 1996. However, the severity of the problem went back to New York and the consent decree, as it is quoted. An FDA report —dated February 10, 1997—called *A Consent Decree Correspondence*, stated, "Because of the serious nature of improper testing, the FDA has no assurance that blood samples from September 1, 1991, through November 20, 1996, were properly tested." If the newspaper's account was off by three years, all the calculations were off. Over one hundred thousand people may have been involved.

Another letter—dated January 14, 1997—stated, "Appropriate follow-up, i.e. recall, should be conducted on blood products from donors for which samples cannot be obtained for retesting." An FDA article dated December 29, 1993, stated, "Greater New York Blood Program Recalls Blood Products." The FDA had received inquiries concerning a recall of blood products by the Greater New York Blood Program in New York City. The blood products— which initially tested reactive for the HIV antibody, the virus that causes AIDS — were not tested in duplicate, as required by the manufacturer's testing instructions and FDA regulations. "The recalled blood products were collected on March 15, 1987, and included red blood cells, platelets (cryoprecipitate blood component used to aid clotting), and recovered plasma. The donor responded that he had tested HIV-1 positive in April 1992."

It appears that the tainted blood problems began well before 1994. It was understandable that they did not want to alarm the public, but it was their duty to inform those who received dirty transfused blood. While the FDA and NYBC communicated their concerns to one another, the blood supplier and owner of the blood products sent to the hospitals did not alert the individuals or the public in a timely manner. One assumes that there were many reasons, but none would be a viable excuse. The *Advincula* case, which was being appealed in the Illinois Supreme Court, makes one think it was all about money. That case concerned an individual infected with tainted blood and was being heard when the consent decree was filed, announcing a recall of the tainted blood products. The *Chicago Tribune* ran the article almost two years later, stating that approximately forty thousand people may also have been infected by tainted blood before the recall. If the recall had been made public in a timely manner—right after November 20, 1996—it would have given that pending case a boost. Other lawsuits might have followed, but because of the late recall, the statute of limitations was running out for many potential victims. It would have been a shattering blow to the blood banks, the hospitals, doctors, nurses, and blood donors. The clock was ticking for me.

I began contacting lawyers about my suspicions and was told that the statute of limitations would soon run out. If I wanted to take legal action against the hospitals, I would have to file a complaint by March 25, 1999. As I prepared my case, I encountered many inexplicable events. I uncovered an interesting fact from the Illinois Department of Public Health: In 1981, only four cases of AIDS were reported. According to their documents, an additional twenty-six thousand AIDS cases had been reported between the years 1982 and 2001. Some were related to tainted blood transfusions, and the majority came from the Chicago area. From 1990 to 1999, 15,643 cases of AIDS had been reported in Cook County and Chicago.

During the tainted blood crisis between 1990 and 1996, there had been an escalation of AIDS cases. In 1990, 942 cases were reported, rising in 1994 to 2,462, and dropping to 962 in 1998. The Illinois Department of Public Health printed statistics on *Reportable Communicable Disease Cases, 1990–1999,* which lists hepatitis A in 1990 at 1,726 cases, and in 1999 at 849 cases. It also states that hepatitis B was at 591 cases in 1990, and at a low of 213 cases in 1999. There was an increase in diseases associated with hepatitis and AIDS/HIV in Cook County during the consent decree era. The hepatitis numbers also decreased dramatically after the 1996 blood recall. I wrote a letter to the Illinois Department of Public Health, requesting an investigation of my mother's death and the blood contamination. In a letter dated April 20, 2001, they responded.

Dear Mr. Slaughter:

Director John R. Lumpkin, M.D. has asked me to respond to your letter of March 14, 2001, regarding complaint number 00-2448. A review of your complaint has determined that it should be investigated under the Illinois Hospital Licensing Act [210 ILCS 85].

As of July 1, 2015, I have not received a resolution of my complaints and inquiries. I have made several attempts to learn the status of my request, but to no avail. The statistics should have encouraged the Illinois Department of Public Health to investigate my complaint.

As I continued to investigate the cause of Mom's death, I became more and more convinced that it was related to the blood transfusions, and not a heart condition. Her medical records, blood tests, and the kidney biopsy, along with advice from a medical professional, supported my belief.

I became more determined to take legal action against the hospitals and those responsible. I met with many attorneys between December 1998 and March 1999, attempting to find someone who would take the case. All of the firms I contacted declined. They said it was because of the complexity of the case and the lack of time in which to prepare before the statute of limitations ran out. I spent hundreds of hours researching legal opinions and documents related to my case. As March approached, my energy levels elevated. Often while researching, I would feel a rush of energy; and then out of the blue, I'd locate an item that proved very important in supporting my theory. I logged hundreds of hours at public and law libraries, seeking answers and guidance on how to prepare the case myself if I were unable to retain a lawyer in time. I believed that many of the attorneys I approached feared taking on the blood bank's attorneys.

Epiphany or Sin

On March 23, 1999, two days before the expiration of the statute of limitations, I filed a complaint in the United States District Court, Northern District of Illinois Eastern Division. It was assigned case number 99 C 1888; I felt like a new attorney filing his first case.

While putting the case together, it felt like unknown forces were guiding me. However, as the first court date approached, I was still looking for an attorney to represent me. A small number of attorneys considered taking on the case, but I could not wait for them. I had to make sure all of the defendants in my case were properly served with summons. After I had the defendants served, I contacted an attorney who had been handling a real estate matter for me, and I told him about the case I had filed.

A few days later, he told me he was interested in handling the case. He assured me that he had handled these types of cases before, and he appeared excited about it. He filed his appearance with the federal court so he would appear as the attorney of record. I didn't think anything was out of the ordinary until one night, a few days before our court appearance in May of 1999, a message was sent to me in a dream, telling me that this lawyer had dismissed the real estate case he was handling for me without my knowledge. This message, I believe, was warning me that my current case was in jeopardy as well. It appeared transcendental, and when I later doubted this dream, a physical object actually moved by itself. A calendar fell off the wall for no discernible reason. I was baffled and somewhat fearful of what I'd seen. After checking with the courts, I learned that the lawyer had dismissed the real estate case in 1998. I was even more baffled and became very angry. My attorney, Mr. Jordan, had called me in February of 1999, indicating on a voicemail message that the real estate case was to go on trial soon.

At that point, I knew there was something to my dreams. I decided not to tell Mr. Jordan that I knew about the case dismissal until I met him in court the following day. I did not want any more surprises. I arrived early at the federal court building to ensure that everything was on track. I wore a blue suit and carried a black briefcase. I looked more like an attorney than my lawyer. At nine-thirty in the morning, we were in court. A few minutes later, the clerk called my case, *Slaughter v. New York Blood Center et al.* There were about twenty-two people sitting in the courtroom, and except for four people, they all stood and approached the bench. I was amazed that all the defendants' lawyers had appeared. Some defendants had two lawyers representing their doctors and hospitals. I knew I was in for a legal battle. I had a choice to make—to quit, or to keep fighting. I had spent almost all of the remaining insurance money on this case, and I had a lawyer I didn't trust. My mind wandered as the judge spoke and the attorneys answered. They spelled their names for the court reporter. One defense lawyer, wearing a very expensive suit, looked toward me and attempted to intimidate me by saying aloud, "I am going to blow this case away." He stared directly at me for about ten seconds. I was on the verge of quitting, feeling powerless fighting all of these defendants alone, but instead I said, "Oh, God, please help me." I began to feel strong again; his attempts to intimidate me only encouraged me to keep fighting. From then on, I never feared the defendants or felt intimidated again.

When the attorneys finished speaking, the judge said, "I know the motions to dismiss will be many, so please don't wait until the last minute." He set the next status hearing for June 16, 1999. I sat down to gather my thoughts and asked myself, "Why didn't I fire this attorney while at the bench?" As I left the courtroom, I saw my attorney down the hall, in a quiet corner, talking with a few of the defendants' lawyers. I was too upset to approach him, but it appeared from their facial expressions that they didn't want me to know what they were discussing. I then believed my dream entirely. My attorney had told me I didn't have to appear and that he would handle everything. Had "handling everything" included selling out? My attorney's actions were now obvious.

A few days later, my attorney told me he needed some money for working on this case. I told him we needed to meet and change our agreement. While at his office, I presented him with an agreement that said, "Our agreement was on a contingency basis when you took over this case." Why was he suddenly asking for money? It was a surprise to me, especially when he knew I was aware of the contingency agreement. Attorney Jordan quickly signed the agreement and asked, "Do you have a check for me?" I told him I would call him later and quickly left his office.

On June 15, 1999, I received a call from the federal court stating there would be no court on June 16, 1999. The judge dismissed the case for lack of jurisdiction in federal court, which extended my statute of limitations by one year. I began to feel more powerful. My prayer, spoken in the courtroom, had been answered. I now had one year to refile the case in the Illinois Circuit Court in Cook County. Attorney Jordan, realizing I was onto his game, filed a motion to remove himself from the case; the judge, though, stated that in his opinion it was a moot issue, because the case had been dismissed. I began to feel strong again. I met with several lawyers and eventually signed a new deal with one of them.

This lawyer was crafty. He was so impressed by my investigation into the tainted blood supplies and my court filings that he attempted to put me on his payroll. He had me investigate an asbestos case. I would receive a percentage if the case was settled or won in court.

I later decided to have my first attorney, Mr. Jordan, investigated by the Illinois Attorney Registration and Disciplinary Commission (ARDC) for dismissing my real estate case without permission. However, he convinced the ARDC that he had done it with my full knowledge. I was bitter that he had gotten away with it, but I learned a great deal about him. I also had the doctor and cardiologist investigated. I knew that unless I could conclusively establish that the blood was tainted, it would be very difficult to prove any wrongdoing by the doctors and the hospitals. I continued to research medical records, court documents, and FDA documents, hoping that the Illinois Department of Public Health would initiate their own investigation and provide a finding that would be useful to me. I continued to write to the Illinois Department of Public Health, and they repeated that it was under investigation. It became obvious, after a while, that they were not looking into it seriously. They said they would, but did they? I knew I would have to refile my complaint within a few months; the filing deadline was quickly approaching.

My new attorney told me he would handle it. Looking back at his actions, I believe he had planned to watch me work; he never intended to file. As the date neared, I reminded my attorney about the statute of limitations. We met at his office more often. Still, he did nothing, and I eventually terminated his services.

A month before I had to refile, in a low mood, I contacted the blood supplier and asked if they wanted to settle the case. I informed the company's lawyer, who was also their vice president, that I had fired my attorney and was representing myself. A few days later, I received a written offer of $10,000 to settle the case. I knew that if I took the money, no further legal action against any of the defendants would be possible. I almost took it; I could have recovered some of the money I had spent preparing the case.

After sleeping on it, I decided not to accept. This story had to be told one day, and I would have been letting my mom and the other victims down. I told the blood supplier's attorney that I was not taking his offer. I filed the case pro se in the circuit court and began to search for another attorney. Like the rest I had contacted, they thought the case was too much work, with no guarantees. I wasn't about to do what I had done in the federal court, which was serve all the defendants and be in the same position all over again. I continued to pressure the Illinois Department of Public Health and search court records.

I was surfing the Internet when I found a very interesting case. A wrongful death case involving a blood transfusion had been appealed to the Illinois Supreme Court. There was a lot of bad press about Justice Freeman, who wrote the opinion—something to do with donations and appointments to the bench. It appeared the medical and justice systems were flawed.

Former governor George Ryan of Illinois was indicted in December 2003 on unrelated charges, which made me more skeptical. Was the state going to investigate my complaint about the tainted blood and the recall? It was also imperative to note that former vice chairman of the Health Facilities Planning Board, Stewart Levine, who had been appointed by Governor Ryan, was indicted in May 2005, accused of leveraging his post on the Board of Health so two of his associates could get lucrative hospital construction and financing contracts. He was also a key fundraiser for the attorney general, who lost his bid to replace the indicted governor. I called the lawyer who handled the case in the Illinois Supreme Court and asked if she was familiar with the tainted blood scare in New York that had affected the Chicagoland area or United Blood Services, and the consent decree that had been signed around the time the Illinois Supreme Court heard her case. She said no. Maybe the recall announcement had been delayed to allow that case to proceed, not letting the plaintiff learn of the tainted blood or decree. If the blood recall had appeared in the newspapers in 1996, the justice's opinion might have been different and opened up a floodgate of lawsuits. By waiting two years, the statute of limitations was over for many, and most of the victims would have died.

It appeared "something" or "someone" was leading me to more and more information. If I hadn't believed in the supernatural and hadn't had that earlier experience with the spirit in Hollandale, maybe my mind would have been closed. I would not have followed up on, or trusted in, any of the dreams or hunches that led me to facts and documents that helped me to investigate this case—such as the property case dismissal. Were the hospitals and blood bank responsible for a massacre? If so, then it was a devastating event. Was there a cover-up? I don't know. Review the FDA Consent Decree, the FDA summary of findings, and other related material, and decide for yourself. The answers to some questions may be found within these documents. I am convinced, from what I have read and reviewed, that there was a massacre, a cover-up, and that similar problems occurred elsewhere in this country without the public's knowledge.

The Smoking Gun is the chronological order of events and sins that will further explain what caused thousands of deaths, including Mom's death. There are numerous letters and correspondences detailed in my journal, *The American Genocide*. A terrible tragedy occurred when hospitals around the country administered tainted blood. It led to indictments and the firing of high-ranking employees at the New York Blood Center. The news appeared in the papers roughly two years after the fact, in the form of a blood recall in the Chicagoland area, where approximately forty thousand people may have been contaminated. I believe there were motives for a cover-up, and I have documented many of the events that took place. I recount public information, documents from the courts, FDA statistics, as well as my mother's medical records. I detailed how many people may have been affected, my attempt to file a class action lawsuit, and situations that may indicate that there was a cover-up and covered coincidental and/or suspicious activities during the recall of 1996.

The lengthy legal battle of *Advincula v. UBS* might explain why I had little to no success fighting in court, and why the chances of success in administrative proceedings were even less. That case also presents a rationale as to why so many attorneys feared a legal battle with UBS and the blood banking industry. I was surprised when, in 2004, I read a story about a yearly ceremony attended by some Illinois supreme court justices and the defendant's leading law firm having a great time together. But I consider it a victory for the victims and me, because I am able to bring this story and information to the public, expressing my right of free speech with no intention to profit financially. If you believe in what you do and enjoy your relationship with destiny, then you will understand why I was driven to tell this story. This story was not only written for my mom, it was written for those we can't hear, those silent voices that belonged to our mothers, fathers, family members, friends, or associates who received tainted blood transfusions.

It's necessary that my readers remember the important points that led me to believe that murder, a massacre, and cover-up may have occurred.

1. There was a blood recall in the Chicagoland area (*Tribune* December 1998).
2. The Illinois Department of Public Health records indicated an increase in AIDS between 1992 and 1996.
3. Over forty thousand people were affected in the Chicagoland area (*Tribune* December 1998).
4. Individuals were indicted for allowing the blood supply to be adulterated.
5. Some of the suspected tainted blood supply was sent to several Chicagoland hospitals over a period of years and went undetected (FDA Consent Decree 1996).
6. NYBC stated, "Recall is being conducted due to our inability to assure that these products were properly tested for the viral markers and anti-HCV, anti-HBC, and HIV p24 antigen" (NYBC July 14, 1997).
7. "We recommend patients be notified if transfused, with any transfusable noted on the attached anti-HCV recall list" (NYBC July 14, 1997).
8. A letter of intent to revoke their license was sent to United Blood Services (UBS) of Chicago. UBS violations included "collection of blood from unsuitable individuals and reinstatement of ineligible HIV-reactive donors" (FDA July 17–September 25, 1995).
9. A consent decree ordering the recall and correction of errors (FDA December 1996).
10. Blood Systems, Inc., had duplicate donors in their computer files (FDA July 17–September 25, 1995).
11. FDA refused to turn over deleted information (FOIA Request 2001).
12. NYBC records indicate the problem was from 1991 to 1996 (FDA Consent Decree 1996).

13. Settlement offers from Blood System, Inc., and Mr. Harper of South Shore Hospital (1999).

14. Illinois Department of Public Health delayed investigation of hospitals (IDPH April 2001).

15. The *Advincula* case heard at the Illinois Supreme Court during the blood recall recommendation. The recall was announced two years later (December 1996).

16. Stuart Levine, the former vice chairman for the Illinois Health Facility Planning Board, was indicted. Former Governor George Ryan appointed him (IDPH 2005).

17. Former Governor George Ryan was quoted as saying his administration "had a culture of corruption" (December 2003).

18. Except for the first complaint against South Suburban Hospital, all the Illinois State Department agencies I had filed a complaint with "let the lawyers off the hook", didn't investigate the hospitals as they stated they would, and failed to properly investigate the doctors involved. All agencies had Governor George Ryan's name on their stationery, and he appointed the State Department heads. This was his administration.

19. The Illinois Supreme Court justice who issued the opinion in the case of *Advincula v. United Blood Services* was once under investigation by the FBI (July 2002).

20. Columbus Hospital stated Mom was diagnosed with Wegener's granulomatosis (November 1996), but their doctor didn't list it as a cause of death (March 1997), although she was under his care and on medication for Wegener's granulomatosis when she died. Columbus Hospital eventually closed down.

Elvis Slaughter

I am hopeful that these findings will encourage you to consider the facts. If you believe a friend or loved one may have been affected and wish to seek answers, below are a few suggestions:

1.   Ascertain if he or she received a blood transfusion between the years 1991 and 1996, or in 1997. I believe there might have been adulterated blood supply at some hospitals after 1996. If death was recent, it may have been from a similar incident.
2.   Look at the blood test results before and after the transfusion. Many transfusions are also given during surgery.
3.   If that person had a setback or died after a transfusion, go a little further and look at the biopsy, autopsy, and/or death certificate for cause of death. Pay close attention to parts 1 and 2 on the death certificate.
4.   If you suspect foul play, you may want to consider an expert opinion. If there was a sudden death while hospitalized, renal failure, sepsis, or suspicious infection in the blood, you might have something.

Below, find a summary of an article from a local newspaper listing hospitals in the Chicagoland area.

Hospitals affected in the Chicago area

Chicago
1.   Bethany Hospital
2.   Children's Memorial Hospital
3.   Chicago Osteopathic Hospital
4.   Columbus Hospital
5.   Edgewater Hospital
6.   Grant Hospital

7.   Louis A. Weiss Memorial Hospital
8.   Mercy Hospital and Medical Center
9.   Norwegian-American Hospital
10. Northwestern Memorial Hospital
11. Rush-Presbyterian-St. Luke's Medical Center
12. St. Anthony Hospital
13. St. Elizabeth's Hospital
14. St. Francis Cabrini Hospital
15. St. Joseph Hospital
16. South Shore Hospital
17. Swedish Covenant Hospital
18. University of Chicago Hospital
19. University of Illinois Medical Center

Suburbs
1.   Condell Memorial Hospital, Libertyville
2.   Gottlieb Memorial Hospital, Melrose Park
3.   Great Lakes Naval Hospital, Great Lakes
4.   Hinsdale Hospital, Hinsdale
5.   Little Company of Mary Hospital, Evergreen Park
6.   Midwest Regional Medical Center (formerly American International Hospital), Zion
7.   Oak Park Hospital, Oak Park
8.   St. Francis Hospital, Blue Island
9.   Victory Hospital, Waukegan

(*Chicago Tribune*, Ken Marshall, FDA, December 2, 1998) Sources: United Blood Service, American Association of Blood Banks, LifeSource, U.S. Food and Drug Administration.

Epilogue

It is fitting to say that like most accusations, this one is legally referred to as "alleged". I am not trying to hurt anyone personally or professionally, nor am I trying to imply that anyone or any company named in this story committed any wrongdoing. I merely ask you to look at the facts and draw your own conclusions.

I am recording what I experienced, heard, felt, read, and believed to have occurred. I don't believe the FDA was part of a cover-up or culture of corruption. I think the FDA did an excellent job with their investigation by means of the consent decree, indictments, inspection of blood companies, and making limited records available to the public. Agencies or bureaus that large will sometimes have difficulties communicating with each other. After reviewing the following headline, "10 On FDA Panel Tied to Drug Firms, Group Claims", I did have some concerns (AP, *Chicago Sun-Times*, February 26, 2005). This article is not related to the tainted blood, but it raises a few questions, especially if this advisory panel had a say in the delay of the recall notification, or if some of its members had ties to the blood banking industry.

31

Elvis Slaughter

A quote, which seems logical, states, "It should be unethical for any judge to accept campaign donations from companies, lawyers, or law firms that have been before them in court." I hope that one day the following questions, and many others, may be answered:

1. Was the blood recall delayed in 1996 for statute of limitations purposes, or to prevent or win a lawsuit?
2. Did more adulterated blood enter the Chicagoland area than reported?
3. Were deaths or illnesses caused by adulterated blood covered up by hospitals?
4. Did the culture of corruption prevent the Illinois Department of Public Health from investigating my complaints? Did it influence the outcome of the doctors' and lawyers' investigations?

Throughout my attempt to find the underlying cause of this matter, not one of the defendants has yet to respond to my request in which I asked them to inform us, Mary's family, whether she had been transfused with adulterated blood from South Shore and Columbus hospitals. There were two settlement offers, one verbally and one in writing, stating, "The settlement will require that you release all claims against Blood Systems, Inc., and other parties who may be involved in this matter" (June 13, 2000).

To the best of my knowledge, no one in the state of Illinois has yet to investigate the recall delay or the cases of an estimated forty thousand patients who received blood transfusions, nor has anyone investigated my mother's circumstances.

Below are a few more items to consider before coming to a conclusion:

1. The suspected tainted blood was sent to hospitals in Chicago and other areas.
2. My mother received blood transfusions at two of these hospitals.
3. She became sick after these transfusions and subsequently died.
4. The blood recall was announced more than two years after it was detected in 1996.
5. There are motives for why the recall was delayed.
6. There are motives for why hospital boards didn't investigate.
7. On February 2, 1997, Mary was diagnosed at South Suburban Hospital with leukopenia and granulomatosis. *Wegener's granulomatosis* was later handwritten next to *granulomatosis*, which gives rise to suspicion. The consulting physician was Dr. Kumarajah, and the referring physician was Dr. Rao.
8. Leukopenia is associated with many of the viruses reported in the blood recall. Granulomatosis is associated with viral infections. Dr. Rao was treating Mom with three types of medications, according to her medical records, prior to her being admitted to South Suburban Hospital.
9. The medical journal indicated that the medicines should not be taken together. Two of the medications suppress the immune system. The medical journal stated two of the medications should not be given to a patient with kidney problems. She developed a kidney malfunction after her body was invaded by severe infections after receiving the blood transfusions.
10. She was placed on dialysis while hospitalized at Columbus Hospital.

11. Dr. Rao is from Columbus Hospital.

Were these medications given to treat and/or cover-up HIV, hepatitis, or leukemia? Were the dialysis and blood transfusions at Columbus given for reasons other than those stated? Was this type of cover-up widespread? Was this genocide?

These are the questions; now we have some answers.

1. One medication treats both leukemia and Wegener's granulomatosis. Wegener's granulomatosis is a noninfectious nephritic syndrome.
2. One medication treats hepatitis. A viral infection associated with HIV, hepatitis, and leukemia was found in Mom's biopsy report.
3. The third medication treats the kidney and organ transplant rejections.

After a Freedom of Information Act request in August 2007, I learned that IDPH failed to investigate my mother's death and that inaction may have caused thousands of patients in Illinois to be in the same predicament as my mom.

For example, when the IDPH statistics reported that HIV/AIDS diagnoses decreased in the mid-1990s, it is believed that HIV/AIDS types of blood transfusion infections were actually increasing; however, the statistics were disguised as deaths related to nephritic syndrome and septicemia. In 1990, IDPH statistics reported there were 1,186 nephritic syndrome deaths. In 2005, IDPH statistics reported there were 2,388 nephritic syndrome deaths and 1,939 septicemia deaths. Many of these infections are believed to have been caused by adulterated blood products that were supplied by blood companies such as United Blood Service (see FDA inspection reports for UBS in Chicago, Illinois, for 1993, 1994, and 1995). An FDA blood recall was announced in Chicago on December 2, 1998. The actual recall date was December 17, 1996, as ordered by a consent decree (FDA Consent Decree 96 Civ. 9464 RPP, December 17, 1996, SDNY), which stated the blood wasn't safe as early as 1991. This recall affected over forty thousand people. These statistical numbers continue to increase every year. A calculation of deaths above the norm from 1990 to 2005 is between thirty thousand and forty thousand in Illinois. This total is similar to the number of people affected by the blood recall.

Dr. Epstein's letter also supports my belief that individuals were infected with tainted blood transfusions before and after the consent decree. Excerpts from the letter of Dr. Jay S. Epstein to Judge Baer concerning *United States v. Maniago and Gonzales* state, "I submit this letter and attached affidavit, to bring to Your Honor's attention the seriousness of the conduct of which defendants Ross Gonzales and Eliazar Maniago have been convicted." Each year, more than 18 million units of blood, platelets, red blood cells, and other blood products are transfused into patients in the United States.

As I am sure the evidence at the trial made clear, adulterating the viral testing of blood donations by manipulating the tests controls and blanks had the effect of making the results of the viral tests in question unreliable. As such, the conduct of which the defendants have been convicted undermined the work of the FDA and blood professionals to ensure the highest possible safety of our blood supply. The FDA has compared the viral testing data from NYBC from before the consent decree with comparable data from the NYBC generated after the entry of the consent decree. This analysis demonstrates that there is an increase in the number of initially reactive tests after the consent decree. This increase is evident for several viral tests. Briefly, we reason that the lower rate of initially reactive tests observed prior to monitoring is an effect of the adulteration.

The defendants, Maniago and Gonzales, were charged with adulterating the blood products and found guilty. They knew their actions, which were thought of beforehand, would kill many Americans. The hospitals and doctors who actually covered up their patients' deaths and diagnoses that were the result of this adulterated blood committed crimes as well.

The facts will speak for themselves.

Final Note

In closing, I can't predict the future outcome for those who are guilty of a crime in this story. One important fact is that some of those who were in key positions to help tainted blood victims now and during the blood recall era failed to perform their duties according to the IDPH's recent statistics on blood poisoning. One thing I am certain of is that many of those linked directly and indirectly to this tragedy have already been punished in some way. There appears to be evidence that their punishment came from a higher level of some kind, and this powerful force will continue to pursue those responsible for their sins.

For example: two former governors were found guilty of corruption; an Illinois Department of Public Health facility planning board member plead guilty to corruption and has implicated many others in a corruption scheme; a lawyer linked to the former chief justice has several pending federal criminal charges; and Columbus Hospital closed down. A tragic auto accident also struck one of the doctors' family members, according to a newspaper article. I am convinced justice will continue to prevail. You may now understand why it is my divine appointment to tell my mom's personal story, which may be linked to current HIV/AIDS blood concerns, now affecting between 33.4 and 46 million people globally (<u>UNAIDS</u>, "Overview of the global AIDS epidemic," *2006 Report on the Global AIDS Epidemic,* PDF [2006]).

Granddaughter's Memory

Mary was my paternal grandmother, born and raised in Mississippi on a plantation. She migrated to Chicago with her children in the early sixties and worked as a seamstress to make ends meet. Her impact on my life started at my birth and lasts through the present.

My fondest memories of my grandmother were when I was a young child. It was then that I learned that work and pleasure could go hand in hand. She started out with blank canvases, scraps of fabric, and ended with functional art, practical art. She enjoyed the process almost as much as the final product.

I remember watching her use her sewing machine on the weekends. She was so graceful and possessed so much control of her craft. I thought she would be tired of making garments and bedding for work, but she continued to do so for pleasure. Sometimes, she would let me help.

I remember picking out fabrics at the store or from her collection and using her sewing machine to create anything I wanted. I wanted to emulate my grandmother in many respects. My creations for myself were not too great, but my dolls and Barbies had more outfits than I could keep up with.

From these types of experiences, Grandmom taught me to be creative, no matter how much fabric I had to work with. She taught me to take a hands-on approach and attempt what I love to do, even if I was not a seamstress. Translating these methodologies to every facet of my life has had a huge and unquestionable impact. I view education with my eyes and learn best with my hands, when capable. Teaching should be done when the teacher has approached what they, in fact, love to do.

My grandmother taught me that when life gives you fabric scraps and a bunch of needles, you should sew the scraps together. She taught me not to worry about getting poked, that eventually I would get better. This has helped me to avoid defeat when things get overwhelming by exhibiting patience and persistence. Make sense of your life experiences, accept them, and make something useful out of them.

My grandmother taught me so many important lessons and skills, but most notably to use my hands and to hold strong interest in what I do. This has carried over to the present and will be the foundation of the career I have chosen. I have the ability to use my hands in dentistry and to be creative and clever, and to compose art which has functionality and practicality. My grandmother has taught me to be open to learning and to explore what I am taught. Because of this, I will be a continuous learner so that I can best serve my patients and my field. And when I educate, I will do so because I truly love what I am teaching, or at least love to teach it.

I will make mistakes, but I have been taught to learn from them and to get over them. I will embrace these lessons; I will continue to grow with these lessons and employ them in every facet of my life, including my dental career.

Dr. Loni N. Slaughter

About the Author

E. Slaughter, Sr., holds a master's degree in criminal justice and corrections from CSU, Chicago, Illinois. Slaughter has over thirty years' of experience in criminal justice and law enforcement, including investigation training. He is a part-time consultant, community activist, and past president of the Illinois Academy of Criminology.

He is the author of *The American Genocide*, *Ghosts of Hollandale*, *The Malcolm X Project*, and publisher and co-author of *Uncle Percy's Blessing*, with his daughter, Loni N. Slaughter.

You can contact the author for additional information by e-mail at eslaugh108@aol.com, or via regular mail at P.O. Box 314, Calumet City, Illinois, 60409.

"I will go before you and make the crooked paths straight; I will break in pieces the gates of bronze and cut the bars of iron." (Isaiah 45:2)

"Therefore understand today the Lord your God is **He who goes before you as a consuming fire. He will destroy them and bring them down before you;** so you shall drive them out and destroy them quickly, as the Lord has said to you." (Deuteronomy 9:3)

"**The Lord will fight for you**, and you shall hold your peace." (Exodus 14:14)

"In Him we have redemption through His blood, the forgiveness of our trespasses, according to the riches of His grace." (Ephesians 1:7)

"But when these things begin to take place, straighten up and lift up your heads, because your redemption is drawing near." (Luke 21:28)

Love
When You
Least Expect It

HEART
SONG

Heartsong Publishing
A Division of Micro Publishing Media

Micro Publishing Media
PO Box 1522
Stockbridge, MA 01262
www.micropublishingmedia.com
info@micropublishingmedia.com
Printed in the United States of America

ISBN 978-1-944068-57-8

2017
Cover and Book Design: Jane McWhorter

Love
When You
Least Expect It

POEMS OF LONGING, LOVING AND LIFE

by William Stevenson

Dedicated To My Beloved Joan

ACKNOWLEDGMENTS

Thank you Deborah Herman, my dedicated and loyal publisher; Joshua Adams, my talented editor; and Jane McWhorter, my wonderful, patient graphic artist, for breathing life into my dormant gift.

And of course you, my reader, love all, love true!

Part One

IN MY YOUTH

Life

My throat was parched and vision blurred. My body burned from within, dry and cracked. "Water, water. . ." I weakly cried, in hope of being heard by anyone or anything. I staggered onward, seeing nothing but the hot, scorching desert as far as the eye could see. Nothing but a mass of wasteland, a horrible, never-terminating land of agony and torture for an unprepared soul who dared challenge it.

I wandered aimlessly hoping to discover water to take away this pain. I didn't know in what direction would lie the blessed fluid to save me from a horrible fate. I tried not to think about my suffering. I thought of a beautiful waterfall, a thousand feet high, and dreamed of the spray splashing on my face. I saw myself falling into the bubbling water below the towering falls, drinking, drinking, drinking.

I can't walk another step–I can't take this agony. "Water! Please God, water!" I fell forward, my face driven into the burning sand. I immediately fainted into a nightmarish sleep with demons all about me. They were hideous creatures too horrible to describe. I lied prone for an unknown amount of time before I realized something odd; the upper portion of my face, including my nose and forehead were not touching the sand. My chin and mouth were pressed against the sand, but the rest of my face was free. I slowly opened my eyes and found myself looking into a hole about three-feet deep. At the bottom was a puddle of water. I cupped some in my hands and drank, soothed and alive.

Death

The sea caresses the cool sand and retreats into the reflection of the moon, only to return again and again, washing the waiting shore. I stood among the shells and timber, wind drying my weary body. The gulls, oddly quiet, were gliding in the moonlight–their silhouettes streaking by.

My spirit felt calmed and collected as I surveyed the horizon, unable to soak in its expanse. I felt as though God was everywhere. Here, truly, was nature's dominion. I turned to my right and saw a shadow stepping closer. Even at that distance she was beautiful to me. I began walking towards her, heart pounding in my temples. I wanted to be close to her. As she approached me, I gently tugged at her arm and with all the love and tenderness in my heart, I kissed her.

Her hair was long and soft, waving in the ocean breeze. A black-bathing suit housed a soft slender body with a white towel draped over her shoulders. She took my hand in hers and we walked silently along the empty beach.

We walked for a long time and never grew weary. It was effortless and liberating. Why we continued walking I wasn't sure, and I didn't need to ask. We simply followed this shared feeling, drawn like a luna moth to its mate. After a time we approached a white, wooden arch that seemed to touch the sky. In spite of its height, we could read the inscription on top. It read: THE KINGDOM OF HEAVEN.

To Life

Here's to life and life in general,
Here's to people large and small,
Here's to problems, questions, and answers,
And here's to egotists who think they have it all,

I love to live and do things well,
I do try my best.
Then there's to those who try not at all
And judge what's poor and best.

Can you imagine such audacity?
Think of how little we know,
So, praise be to Almighty God,
Praise Him continually.
Forever!

I don't think he controls us,
He lets us travel our meager ways,
Sometimes when we need him,
He's there.

Egotism

This is a world of egotists,
Everyone looking out for themselves.
We can't see past our nose,

That's what makes our country strong.
Can you imagine that?
Everyone looking out for themselves.

Let's face it,
When it comes down to it
We help others to help ourselves.
Unless…

Secret Of Life

Be aware of limpid, lifeless love,
Even if it hurts,
Stay on your guard and keep your mind alert
So you can judge without the cloud of hope.
Take all life and resolve that life is life.

The secret of life is: leave it alone.
Don't search for happiness and wishful dreams,
You won't find the best and you'll just take what is left
Grudgingly, because the weary searching is a fog,
A smoke screen.

My suggestion is, look to your Maker,
He'll show you peace of mind and happiness,
Purpose and gratitude,
And remember, whatever happens to you,
You can always talk to Him and rest your soul.

Finding Joy

When I have reached the peak of life,
I'm sure I'll feel as I do now.
If I could grab the earth,
I'd still be miserable.

Joy is not found in power and wealth.
Joy is found in love and health.
So, I will pray for health and you
And hope the Lord will see me through.

Goals

My goal is a mountain climber's dream,
The tallest peak anywhere.
One can go no higher.
But I am amongst ant mounds,
Lower than any around.
One can go no lower.

Dying

I wonder what it's like to die.
One never knows when it's time to go.
Mr. Death never tells you so.
He sneaks in one day and you're done.

You can't see him or hear him, yet
The mark he leaves on those left behind,
Is etched in stone,
You know when he's paid a visit.

He doesn't care if you are young
To him, there is no bias to the well-aged,
Because when it's time, he ends the page.
And, when your book is done, you're God's.

Were we not before?
Dying is a consolation, friends,
Because once you die, you die no more,
And you can open one other door.

Alone

Void, dark, empty, vain, insincere is life.
I am alone.
Thunder, lightning, downpour
All crashing down on me at once.

Run! Run! Oh, God, hurry.
But where? Quick! Where?
That noise, that rumbling, that smashing.
It's silence. Run, you fool, run.

Brave Weakling

Consider life and you are brave,
Consider yourself and you are weak.
You are also average.
Do we esteem ourselves before our task?
Or, should we find our niche and crawl into it
While the rest of the world seals us in,
To be overlooked, as they think they run the world,

But I must ask,
What the hell are we doing here?
Who are we?
Why are we?
Are we a purpose, or do we live a
Comedy for another race or group
To laugh at? Must it always be a joke?

Optimism

I approach every new day
With renewed expectation.
Hoping, wishing, praying
Every day with increased anxiety.

Surely, today is the day.
Surely, there will be no more worrying.
Or waiting, Oh well, probably tomorrow or
No longer than the weekend.

I approach every new week
With renewed expectation
Hoping, wishing, and praying.
Surely.

Self Pity

Don't let them see your face,
Your tired, crying, tear-stained face.
When you reveal it,
You show your broken, beaten heart.
Oh, heart, the weight you must bear.
Oh, poor little defenseless heart
But you'll keep on pounding away
And, I'll keep on living.

Growing Up

Yesterday I killed ten of me,
Today, I'll kill ten more.
Sun up tomorrow, I'll hang up my gun
To find another kind of fun.

I think I'll be a fireman
And be a tribute to fellow man,
I'll ride the streets and ring my bell,
And save the people from their hell.

Or, maybe I'll be an Injun
And catch a big white pigeon.
I'll use his feathers for my hat
To show the people where I'm at.

The trouble behind my indecision
Is the lack of recognition,
I'm a little boy, you know
And I need love to help me grow.

Being A Kid

When it rains, we stay at home.
When it shines, it's time to roam.
Over hill and over dale,
Or over great oceans we will sail.

We will fight ten thousand men
And when it's over, we will have won,
Or, we will sail the seven seas
Or fly up and glide in the breeze.
Isn't it fun to be a little kid?
We can find a treasure anywhere.
There's nothing we can't do,
Don't you wish you were little, too?

A Few Ditties

I wonder what it's like to die,
I wonder what makes people cry,
I wonder what makes airplanes fly,
Why do I always wonder why?

I can tell that it's spring
Because I hear the robins sing.
I can see the grass and leaves,
And the roses make me sneeze.

Humanity

What a strange life people lead.
A mass of egotists groping around in darkness.
They know so little, they feel that much.
I'd rather be dead than average.
Sir, what is your interest besides yourself and your purse?
Are you curious about the button you push? Again and again.
Do you think there's more to life than your worldly desires?
Please, don't give me your disappointing answers–again.
I've been hurt enough.

Alone II

I'm all alone in love tonight,
I need you close to me.
I'll dream a dream of you
My sweet, and hope you'll dream one too.

I'm all alone in sorrow dear,
I love you constantly.
I cannot be without your love,
You're like the sky above.

Above us always it is there,
Just like my love for you.
It won't subside,
I need you by my side.

Missing

If I don't see you before you leave
I'll see you in my dreams.
I'll think of you always and wonder, too,
If you you're thinking of me as I of you.

I'll miss you this summer,
I'll want you by my side,
I'll pray for you this winter,
And hope you'll always love me.

I can't understand the way you are,
I can't understand the things you say,
I can't understand the things you do,
I only understand that I love you.

Victory

No need to tell me that I'm wrong,
No need to make me understand,
No need to say, "It isn't right-
"To need you as the beach needs sand."

Don't try to show me your way,
Don't try to make me see light,
Don't try to push me away,
Nothing can save you from this plight.

This love of mine cannot be wrong
Because my dreams feel so true,
I'll find you always near my side
Because I'm in love with you.

Disappointment

How should I feel?
Should I dry tear filled eyes and smile? I hope,
Sew up my heart with red string? Nope,
Should I build up new hopes
Only to find the pain they can bring?
Before my very own soul
This is the only love I know.
I've felt this love before and
I don't want it again.

Needing Love

It's a strange thing about me,
I need love.
There is no existence without it.
I'm like a dope addict or alcoholic
I need love like a fix or a drink.
Sometimes I find it, but it never lasts. It runs empty,
But I'm told that love lasts.
Maybe I know no love.
Once you have loved, in love you remain.
I was in love and in love I remained.

Beautiful Feelings

See the picturesque sunset and the hummingbird.
Picture a magnificent mountain and any waterfall.
Inhale the elegant blossoms when spring comes waltzing in
And feel your heart pounding with excitement of a lover's kiss
Think of everything that is enchanting and multiply it by ten
Think of how it can happen again,
You remind me of all these things.
I see your head of hair, and I flutter,
It highlights your funny little nose and rapturous smile.
You cannot be any different than an innocent
Sprite, so full of youth and love.
Your hair is your personality and your life.
It's what I remember first.

Melancholy

The burning desire within my veins is quenched once again
By the cold, cold sea of nonchalance.
My heart had begun to rejoice again, but as days passed
My laughter turned to tears.
Depression engulfs my heart and melancholy grips my brain.
I am so disheartened,
Empty, I can't even cry.

Being Apart

What holds us together?
What keeps our hearts so true?
Why do I write so much?
Three small words, "I love you."

Those silly words, the meaning
Keeps echoing in my ears.
Even though I heard them once,
They'll echo through the years.

And now, I hope and pray
That I will hear them once more,
For the echo does grow dim
And I'd like it as I did before.

You just tell me what you think
And I will tell you too.
You just ask me what I think
And I will say, "Of you."

So, to make it short, my Sweet,
I'd like to hear from you
Those weary words that mean so much
"I really do, I promise you."

Face To Face

Standing hand in hand
With faces to the wind,
We will hold our heads high.
With bodies firmly set in place,
We will face this tired world

Because

As we stand face to face
With our fingers clasped together
And eyes bathed in warm adoration
The world somehow fades away.

Giving

I give to you my inner self
And all my gentleness.
I give to you what you need from me
And all my tenderness.
I give to you my naiveté
And all my wholesomeness.
I give to you the joy of love
And what it means to me.
I give and I receive.
But I do not give enough
My heart tells me so.

How Do I Love Thee

I love you for what you are
And not what you ought to be.
I love you for what I'm not,
Complementing what I don't see.

Not a dream or untarnished hope,
You are you and loved for that.
You are all women and what they'd
Like to be.

You are a woman: sensuous, lovely, scheming,
Warm and conscious of yourself.
You are grace and dignity and
You are tenderness.
You are what you want to be
And you are born to be loved by me.

Metamorphosis

From the first moment I saw you,
I knew you were sui generis,
And I was immediately pleased.
How quickly I became your foremost admirer
As your mind became exposed to me.
What a joy to be with one
Whose thoughts could reach the sky,
Whose mind could wonder why
Like mine.

As time passed, admiration grew to adoration.
The time you've occupied my thoughts,
Almost at once I learned that
The love that adoration brings
Is pure, complete, and resolute.

It grows without water,
How I tried to manifest my love without
Demands or expectations,
Just a need to love.

Then one day the flower burst open to the sun
And, oh, what fulfillment my awe-struck soul had.
Where am I now and where to go
Is so irrelevant.
For I am we and we shall be. Shouldn't we?

Part Two

AMIDST MANHOOD

THE FOREST AND THE GHETTO

Forest

I have always enjoyed quiet walks in the woods
And this one began as any other,
Rustling brush and loose leaves in the wind,
Wisping as it played tag among the trees
Being my elusive companion as I meandered
Around logs and on down trodden branches.

The fragrance of pine was intoxicating,
Sunbeams sliced through the trees
These shafts of light danced with shadow
Flickering faint and picking up again as bright.

Although I walked alone, I wasn't lonely.
The solitude seemed to engulf my soul and
Its soft comfort served as a salve for my jangled nerve endings.
I needed the quiet of nature, slow and safe.

After a while, I sat on the ground with my
Back resting on a nearby tree.
As I relaxed, I listened to the sounds around me.

A mockingbird, entertained all the creatures
Who were listening to his impressive imitations,
A scurrying chipmunk making its way home,
The sound of a brook rushing over stones and upon drift wood.

In this peaceful paradise I closed my eyes and fell asleep.
When I awoke, moments—or hours later—I began my trip back.
But as I walked, I couldn't find the right path or direction.
The way seemed closed to me and I was lost.

The mockingbird was quiet and my elusive companion, left me
And was blowing up a storm.
Dark clouds rushed to cover up the sun and
I knew that it would soon be dark, very dark.

Well, darkness came.
The woods became a horror to me,
A torturous prison from which there was no escape.
I had lost my way, silent and alone.

Ghetto

I always hated the walk home from the subway.
It made me ill.
The streets were littered with garbage and debris.
The dogs left droppings everywhere.
The city's stench was overcoming and far more than I could bear.
Children played in filth, under smog and acid rain.

Unemployed men sat idly on steps drinking cheap liquor
From crinkled brown bags.
Wasting humanity in the Ghetto.

The odors of cooking, grease, and filth greeted me
Each time I entered my condemned building.
The walk up each stair to my apartment conjured up thoughts of
Hell,
As surely I must be close.

Then one day, leaving my flat, I saw you.
You were standing on the sidewalk.
The sun was shining that day and your eyes captivated its light.
My surroundings transformed.
A whisper blew leaves across the yard, tall trees
Creaked and Yawned as a bird rustled in its nest.
You noticed, and the beauty of the forest I once knew so well
Came true.

Is There Darkness In The Sun

(Lyrics To A Song Never Sung)

Lady, Lady in the sun
You reach out to everyone.
Lady, Lady that I see
Will you please reach out to me?

I'm a God-forsaken man,
I'm a God-forsaken man.
I can't stand the world I see,
Will you please reach out to me?

I see the world in its place,
I see the world in disgrace,
It makes me sad as it goes 'round,
There is no peace that I have found.

Crying, sadness everywhere
And more pain than I can bear.
Is there hope for anyone—
Or, is there darkness in the sun?

Gentle Flower In The Sun

Gentle flower in the sun,
My mind caresses your visage,
So soft, so pure
I cannot speak of what you mean to me.
I feel the touch of your breath,
The life that stirs inside.
I cry so that perhaps I can nourish
Growth, but my tears only dampen dirt,
How tender soft that deep caress
I feel when my mind roams,
I speak softly to ease my heart,
And hope you'll know what is inside.
I know, I sense just what you feel.
The hope of all that is within;
The need to be understood.
The hope to be loved as though there
Were no place that love could be;
The hope that love was meant for me.

All Time Is Now

Life is fleeting; only thoughts remain.
The joys of today are tomorrow's sadness
And yesterday's hope is
Today's despair.
Past goodness flees like the wind
And what is now is not related to what was then.
Therefore, I believe that:

All time is now,
Tomorrow is another place.
The special sense of here, of now
Fades into the soul.

Two gentle people reaching out
To find meaning
In themselves must
Suffer for the toll.

Where is tomorrow? For it
Shall pass away.
Where is tomorrow?
I thought its dream was yesterday.

Recapturing A Moment

Softness,
You reach out to me–
No sound is heard
But the patter of your voice.

You are drawn to me,
A pattern of beauty
Marks, ideal and none alike.
I am so drawn to you

In the stillness of a predawn
The evening passed
As a simple courier
Announcing our love to come–
I move towards you and
You towards me, with ample gravity
Our lips met.

Secret Place

I have always had a secret place
Somewhere deep inside myself
From the moment that
I became aware of life's beat.

When buffeted by storms
And existence's unexplained madness,
I would withdraw
To this quiet sanctuary,
Alone and safe.

Now, as I run from the thunder,
I seek that private place and
It's gone.

Woman-Child

I watch you walk with your head held high,
Your long brown hair bouncing on your shoulders.
You are a picture of a woman–
You are all women and what they'd like to be:
So bright and wholesome with
A child's innocence and full-beauty.

Woman-child, I see you and yet, somehow,
I can't believe you are real.
On one hand, you are such a little girl,
And on the other, you're wise beyond your years.
I call out to you with a voiceless hope
And wonder what you think of me.
I whisper softly, so you can't hear,
"Do you think of me?"

How Do You Please Me

How do you please me?
Let me count the ways—
There are so many to enumerate
Where do I start?

Your loving eyes seeking mine
In the stillness of the night;
Your loss of words when deeply moved;
Your precious innocence and your honesty of it;
The artistic way you clothe yourself
With each outfit a painting or a song;
The special way you respond to me–
So honest, trusting, and fond.
And, the special way you make me feel.

These are only just a few
But mostly dear, I am pleased
Because, you are you.

I Believe

I believe,
That if I tried very hard–
I mean real hard,
I could in fact,
Wish a rainbow in the sky.

I feel,
That if I willed with all my might
That somehow, I could
Bring the moon one inch
Closer to the Earth.

I'm certain,
That if given the opportunity,
I could convince
The world leaders
To bring peace to mankind,
If only they'd believe me.

I know, too,
That if God felt
I was in need of Him,
He would appear before my eyes.

I can,
Make small children laugh,
Inspire grown men
To stand up for their convictions,
And make the elderly feel good about age.

I also can,
Instill dignity
In those who need it
And give hope
To those who despair.

But, with all this power and might,
I am enchanted by you.

Alone III

I have had a vision of
A better world to come,
In fact, have tried to make
It into ours now.

It seems so sad that I can't bring
Peace without a war,
But yet, no matter what I try to do,
The battle is at hand.

I am an alien in my own land,
A stranger for these times,
No matter where I go or whomever I see,
There seems no place on this Earth for me.

I have tried to seek sanctuary
From the madness of my life,
And have rediscovered the niche inside myself.
There is no other place where I can reach out and cry,
And so, I must be alone and inside my forest, my ghetto.

New Love

When you appeared as a full moon,
Lighting the darkness of my life,
I began to see the shadows of my world.

I am afraid, because
I know the moon must wane,
Eventually to leave the night sky
And I shall be left in darkness, once again.

Part Three

THE LATTER YEARS BRING LOVE AGAIN

Seeds Of Love

Where you have stepped, I've planted seeds of love,
While you have slept, I've sown them from above,
And so, instead of Antheia's flowers,
They yielded blossoms from my passion's powers.

The fabric of this wondrous life we live
Is woven from the joy our hearts now give.
I'll always love you near and from afield
And promise all the gifts our lives can yield.

I love you now and pledge to raise the score,
Each dawn as you awake, you'll rise to more.
The words I share, my love, come from my soul
And are only meant for you to make you whole.

I Will Try

I can't wash away your years of abuse and being demeaned;
But, I WILL TRY.
I can't erase your years of a troubled childhood;
But, I WILL TRY.
I can't protect you from the guilt visited upon you by your sons;
But, I WILL TRY.
I can't replace the love your sons have for you;
But, I can give you mine.
I can't replace the companionship you enjoy with your girl friends;
Friendship is irreplaceable.
I can't replace the peace you enjoy in your Bettendorf Church;
But, we can add to it with our Bellmore Church.
What I can do is love you like you deserve to be loved.
I can be your sanctuary from loneliness and life's struggles.
After sixty plus years of living a life in which you had no control,
God has given you a choice of how you want to live on,
I hope your choice will include US.
I believe that there is no one on Earth better for you than I,
God gave me a choice, and that is You.
God gave me to you and you to Me.

Sunshine On Your Face

You shall always have sunshine on your face;
My shadow will not fall upon your space.
We shall walk side by side in harmony,
With our life blessed by peaceful reverie.
Your life shall be one of love and respect,
And no day shall pass where you'll know neglect.
You are the purity of our blessed life,
And I shall love you daily as my wife.

A New Beginning

Upon dawn brings a new beginning,
Its light brings the joy of our new love.
As we gaze at our bright new world,
Our future rolls out like a flag unfurled.
I reach out to you, you softly take my hand,
We both go forth to explore our claimed land,
The air smells sweet from the flowering field
As our life's direction becomes revealed,
We are destined to love, honor, and obey,
As we will pledge our love with each new day.

Choices

Your life of family, work, and friends
Is yours to keep as it depends
If this is the life that you seek,
Without my kiss from week to week.
If you have found your happiness,
Make no change, there is no duress.
Enjoy the time that you have set,
Perhaps the best your life can get,
But, if you choose to marry me,
You will find love's legacy.
Haven't we found a love that's true?
Aren't you for me and I for you?

Come Home

We can see our lives are melting away,
Which is an awful price to pay.
We must stop this sacrifice and madness,
It is too long that we've lived with sadness.
There is nothing left for us to gain-
Staying apart is driving us insane.
The time long since has come to set us free;
I must belong to you and you to me.
Pack your bags and make a call upon your phone.
Tell me to come; you're tired of being alone.

Together

We cannot replace your former life,
We can embrace it as husband and wife.
When good, loving people stay together,
They will persevere through all kinds of weather.
Dearest, we have no choice as you can see,
I must be with you; you must be with me.
United we will face what life has in store,
As we need each other and not much more.

Us

Sunshine and rainbows and flowers and bees,
Geese that are honking and puppies that sneeze,
Waves with white foam and grey dolphins at play,
Soft rain on our faces and warm breezes that sway,
Song birds that serenade and kittens that snuggle,
Seagulls that laugh and babies that cuddle,
Soft summer breezes, the sun in our face,
Invites great pleasure in our unique space.
These special joys give us inner peace,
Enhancing our love that will never cease.

Love's Light

The train of your life has pulled into the station,
Is this your last stop in your imagination?
That place in Land port,
You once knew as your last resort.
Now you have seen there is far more ahead,
You no longer must live life with dread,
See that bright light not very far away?
It's my love's light that holds your past at bay.
So, Love, stay on the train and seek the light
That flows from my loving eyes day and night.

Giving

You gave your childhood to your mother, father, and brother
And bore a weight and sadness like no other.
When you escaped to a new domain,
You carried inside, such hurt and pain.

Soon you conceived and gave two sons life
While it was difficult for you to be a wife.
You gave your boys love and your youth,
While no one around knew your truth.

Your heart was heavy and you lived with grief,
As there was no place you go to find relief.
Time passed and yet you gave the boys your middle age,
While you were stuck in place and remained upon their stage.

With your youth gone and your later years too,
You felt a life of love was forever over for you.
But then, a miracle of life took place.
At the age of sixty, God gave you His grace.

While darkness held your past, the future is now bright
As you were blessed with the gift of God's holy light.
Mercy and salvation, He is your rock and core,
With a divine knot, together on angel's wings we soar,

You have always been the woman that God sent to me,
While all around you, sadly, you are seen differently.
You have given your children all that there is to give,
And now it is the time for YOU to live.

My List

My life has almost moved from Act Three to Four,
But before I can move on,
I have a short list
And not one item can be missed.
.

On my list I must inform
All of these folks, who will be forlorn.
First here is a sweet friend, who depends on me,
Above all, she will set me free.

Dearest daughter will be a total wreck,
She'll wish me bon voyage and hug my neck.
My two sons will care less about my fate,
All they will want to do is lock my gate.

The list grows longer and I groan,
As I check one off, another gets added on.
There will always be something in my way
That keeps me from living my bright new day.

So here is what I have decided to do:
CUT MY LIST SHORT SO I CAN BE WITH YOU.

If I Could Make My Fantasies Come True

If I could make my fantasies come true,
This is what I would wish for you:
You would conclude that you have shed your guilt,
And can't gain any more from the life you've built.

You'd see you freely gave away our happiness,
And traded it in for constant stress.
You would realize you gave up much of your dignity
As a border, maid, cook, and a nanny.

You would see you're building a firm for Char,
But gain naught, no matter how good you are.
You'd concede that you've sacrificed privacy
In a small house as a small party of three.

You would clearly see that you will not grow,
As you can't blossom where you cannot sow.
You'd realize you're no Princess on a throne,
Because in the end, you will be all alone.

I dream that you'll break with your demeaning past
'Cause you're aware that life is passing fast.
I hope that you'll begin to sculpt reality
When you see our future isn't fantasy.

My hope is that insights will come to you
As it's revealed you've done all you can do.
My hope is that you'll break out of your pod,
And accept the life given to us by God.

The Domain Of The Princess

In a land three thousand miles away,
The sun shines upon a bright new day
Revealing beauty of land and sea.
Our God has shed His grace for thee.

The sea spills life upon the shore,
Its power lures you close for more.
You can't escape nature's domain,
You're pulled inside and seem to remain,

You stand in awe of all you view–
Visions sculpting you pure and new.
Life and beauty are in the air,
Feelings of love are everywhere.

This land of love is yours for sure,
As all of your ills it will cure.
So, dear, please accept my hand,
Before the gates close to our promised land.

The Gift Of Life

When you gave birth, you gave your son his life.
As time went by, you gave him yours in strife.
Passing judgment on your filial affair
Will cause conflict, not getting us anywhere.
All I can reveal, I hope in the end
That you will feel you did not over spend.
Our time is precious; an amazing gift to give.
Has it made your life easier to live?
What is truth? It's only for you to know.
What is next? It's only for God to know.
Please take back your life and give it to me;
God has given the gift of mine to thee.

Marooned

I am lost in a lonely land,
Misty and shrouded, surrounded
By beaches of white sand.
My warm house is my interlude
From all the stress of solitude.
Those I confront are strange to me,
They don't understand — I can't stand
Being alone, I shiver an emptiness,
As a life eludes you, I strain,
It has to include, not wane,
So daily I gaze upon the sea
For the sight of your trek to me.

My Darling's Do Over

There comes a time for everyone,
When our sad world is filled with strife.
Life as you wish, is not as it seemed,
You wish you could take a step back
So you can get yourself on track.
The right path, a desire to put yourself in clover
And do what we call a 'do over.'

Now that spring is upon our Earth
And Easter, too, for what it's worth,
We find renewal of dreams are here,
The gleam and glint and attraction,
I can't seem to interact and grasp
On to what we hold dear,
I fear our dream is long far, far away
Our life of us is this, shall we stay?

Tears Of Love

Tears produced by the wreckage,
Leak and cascade through cracks,
What has happened to all your hopes and dreams?
Reality is not reason enough,
By God, my dear we've had it rough,
  The joy and romance of life withered,
And murky sadness greeted you each day.
You wonder, "Is this how life ends for me?"
At least I thought because you look lonely,
Or is it I? I swear time is fleeting,
Then your answer came out of the blue,
A shock transformed you.
The angry storm
Faded away and with it all your stress,
Feelings of love filled your heart and your soul
As tears of love were made
Anew and made you whole,
Love tears, you see, were sweet as you imagined and more
As on this day you opened a new door.
Once you walk through it, there is no return.
Through the tears, I hope you learn joy.

Finale

LOVE WHEN YOU LEAST EXPECT IT

The Most Beautiful Place On Earth

The most beautiful place on Earth
Is yours to seek in first-class berth.
If God lived somewhere we could see,
For sure, He'd be found in Hawaii.

As soon as you invoke your plan,
We'll pack our bags and fly the span.
Once we're there amidst rainbows and love,
We'll look on high and thank God above.

Rebirth

Our two souls were separated,
Trapped on separate ships upon an angry sea
As the sting of hopelessness was felt by each.
By magic, the storm subsided and set us free
And deposited us upon an enchanted Hawaiian beach.

The sun was high that day and the wind did race
As the sea caressed the waiting shore.
You and I, with loving gaze, stood face to face
As eye to eye we searched for more.

I reached out to hold your gentle hand
And you responded by holding mine so tight.
Then a bolt from Heaven's mighty sky
Made us lovers with His eternal light.

Our two souls are lost no more—no more in mortal strife,
Together on that day, God's breath created future husband and wife,
Our love triumphed over all in this life,
As He gave us each other to adore.

ABOUT THE AUTHOR

William Stevenson is president of National Tax Consultants, Inc. (a tax preparation and taxpayer representation firm for individuals and businesses). Bill is an Enrolled Agent, a Certified Financial Planner, and earned a Doctorate in Education from Temple University in Educational Administration. In addition, he is one of about 250 professionals since 1943 who has been admitted to practice before the United States Tax Court as a non -attorney.

On a lighter note, Bill is the author of a series of six children's books that are available from Micro Publishing Media, in print and ebook format. The central theme in all the titles is RICKY'S DREAM TRIP. RICKY'S DREAM TRIP TO ANCIENT EGYPT, the third book in the series was awarded the prestigious Readers' Choice Award from Grandparents.about.com, a national online magazine devoted to grand parenting. RICKY'S DREAM TRIP TO COLONIAL AMERICA is the first in the series to be translated into Spanish.

Finally, LOVE WHEN YOU LEAST EXPECT IT, is a book of poetry traversing Dr. Stevenson's journey through longing, loving and life.